Addiction Struggles?

Don Barnes

Published by Don Barnes, 2024.

Table of Contents

About the Author

Don is the founder and author of Life Works in Threes!™ E-books. He is a lifelong Texan who has traveled extensively while taking a keen interest in human behavior. His curiosity about life and what drives humans led him to the discovery of how life works in threes. He coined this term as the *Tryune Concept*.

Don attended college on an athletic scholarship and then embarked on a 30-year career in the oil and gas industry. Since the year 2000, he has been a consultant for distributors and manufacturers of various industries. Along the way, he worked on his Tryune discovery in hopes of someday sharing his findings with those struggling unnecessarily... in life. What Don surmised from 40+ years of R&D was that people were struggling unnecessarily because they were not aware that "life works in threes." They, for the most part, have been living their lives <u>by chance</u> rather than <u>by choice,</u> he also discovered.

From this, he began focusing on the "mechanics of life" which shows formulas for success with subjects such as *life, health, money, purpose and so forth*. When people are able to grasp the Tryune Concept, they can apply the formulas with topics that interest them and begin eliminating the struggle. This epiphany is what triggered his Tryune venture and is now on the path of sharing with all who desire to improve on their lives.

Don currently resides in Southern California and Texas while overseeing his businesses and investments.

Life Works in Threes™

When I was a kid growing up, no one sat me down and said, "Okay Don, I'm going to show you how life works so that you can navigate your way through adulthood." I graduated from school, got married and went about my way with the "learn as you go" concept. It was kind of like putting together a backyard swing set without a set of instructions. Lots of frustration and do-overs, for sure!

My discovery of the "triune" word and noticing how things come together in threes is really what set me off on researching that maybe "life comes in three" ...sort of a mechanical approach to managing life, if you will. I combed the libraries and bookstores for information on this and found one book on the subject that was written back in 1951. The author's name was John S. Arant.

What Mr. Arant had to say is this "For lack of a better name, I have called this *The Triangle of Triumph* and therefore, consistent with the name, since most of these conclusions are built on the geometric figure of the triangle." He continued "All Life and all lives are seated in, and circumscribed by, the triangle. The Author and Source and Director of all life is Himself triune in character – Father, Son, and Holy Spirit. Man is of triple nature – body, mind, and spirit – and within those three there are many triangles – desires, development, decay; intellect, will, sensibilities. Of this "paced interlude in the midst of eternity" which we call time there is the triangle of Past, Present, and Future. Space – that limitless and measureless element of the physical universe – is best known in terms of Height, Breadth, and Depth. Try building yourself some triangles along the lines of your Will, your Work, your Way – You will find some interesting angles.

So, for the first time, I realized that life is designed in a mechanical way to come in threes. That means you don't have to rely on wishing and hoping things turn out okay. You can actually look at the three parts that a particular thing is made of and then apply them to get what you're wanting. Like a three-ingredient recipe or a combination lock. With a combination lock, you need the three exact numbers to unlock the lock...otherwise you will continue to struggle.

Some 40 years later, I accumulated things that work in threes and that's when I knew I needed to share this with anyone wanting answers. To have success/harmony in your life, just apply the three parts of an area you're working on, and things will fall into place. I also learned that the recipe for success with just about anything is by doing these three things, consistently – THINK positively, SPEAK positively and ACT positively. For example, if I want to be a successful artist. I would think to myself "I can do this because I have the talent." Then I would speak it this way "Yes, I am working on my art degree and plan to do portraits professionally." Finally, I would act on that by taking art classes and continue crafting my skill. Eventually, I will see the positive results/ success I'm looking for.

Conversely, if I think positively but speak negatively...it will cancel out. Or if I speak positively but have no positive action going on...nothing will happen.

I looked up "How Life Works" and "The Mechanics of Life" and these are really talking about the biology of how our cells work and other chemistry. TRYUNE WORKS! teaches that life is kind of like building blocks. Pick a topic you may be struggling with. See the three parts that topic consists of and then start applying them...on a consistent basis. That will help you overcome the struggle and get you back in harmony/ success with how life works.

For 30+ years I was a golf instructor (by accident). My two kids had some success playing junior golf and so friends and neighbors would ask me to show them and their kids how to play golf successfully. From all of this, I got pretty good at watching golfers on the driving range and could spot right away why they were struggling with hitting bad golf shots. I was able to do that because I knew the three steps to hitting good golf shots. I learned them from studying golf and played for several decades. I "broke the code" for me so to speak.

So now you know that life works in threes. You can live your life *by choice* rather than *by chance* and that my friend... is the key to a fulfilling life.

LIFE WORKS
IN THREES!

My sanctuary on the Pacific coast

Introduction

Addiction is a complex and chronic condition characterized by compulsive engagement in rewarding stimuli, despite adverse consequences. It often involves the repeated use of substances like drugs or alcohol, but it can also manifest as behavioral addictions, such as gambling or internet use. The fundamental feature of addiction is the inability to control the urge to engage in the behavior or consume the substance, even when it leads to significant harm or distress in one's life.

At its core, addiction alters the brain's chemistry and functioning. When a person engages in an addictive behavior, it triggers the release of neurotransmitters such as dopamine, which are associated with pleasure and reward. Over time, the brain becomes reliant on these substances or behaviors to achieve a sense of well-being, diminishing its natural ability to regulate mood and reward. This leads to a cycle where the individual needs increasingly larger amounts of the substance or more frequent engagement in the behavior to achieve the same effects, reinforcing the addiction.

The impact of addiction extends beyond the individual to affect their relationships, work, and overall quality of life. It can lead to physical health problems, mental health issues like depression or anxiety, and social or legal difficulties. Overcoming addiction typically requires a multifaceted approach, including medical treatment, psychological support, and lifestyle changes. Understanding addiction as a multifactorial issue involving biological, psychological, and social dimensions is crucial for effective intervention and recovery.

My discovery of the Tryune Concept

Before we dive into addiction struggles and how to overcome them, let me share my discovery of the Tryune Concept and how life works in threes. It all began in the summer of 1982.

I grew up with parents who treated everyone with decency and respect. My three older sisters and I were raised in a home that was "middle-class traditional." We lived in modest homes in different small towns, attended school and church on a regular basis and celebrated all the traditional holidays. Eventually we settled during the spring of 1964 in the big city of Houston, Texas. I'll never forget the vastness of the city and hearing sirens from police cars, fire trucks and ambulances on a regular basis. I was excited and scared at the same time.

Once settled in this fast-paced city, I finished my growing-up years with an academic diploma and sweetheart intact. I got a job, bought a car, got married, bought a house and produced two beautiful babies in a span of about 5 years. Talk about having to grow up fast!

Things went from great in my childhood to absolute misery in my young adulthood. I began to struggle with my job because deep down I just hated what I was doing. This problem created a snowball effect because soon after, my weight, my finances, my relationships, my happiness and everything else worth saving was going down the drain. I eventually hit a level of frustration that I had never experienced before and didn't know how to get out of it. My cry for help was for anyone or anything to come to my rescue. I just ran out of solutions for my situation.

This is when my discovery happened.

One night shortly after my meltdown, while sleeping soundly, the word "triune" began to softly pound in my head like a mantra. I woke up a little startled and decided to go look up the word in my favorite dictionary (this was WAY before Google.) The definition said '**triune** (try-une) – 1) a group of three things; united. 2) Being 3 in 1 such as *humans are mental, physical and spiritual.* I scratched my head, got a glass of water and went back to bed.

The next day while driving around town, I began thinking about things that I was taught in my younger years that came in threes. My Boy Scout manual taught that to have **character**, I needed to be *1) physically strong, 2) mentally awake and 3) morally straight.* My high school football coach would say emphatically "If you want to be **a good football player**, you have to be *1) mobile 2) agile and 3) hostile!*" My first sales manager shared with me that to be **a successful salesman**, I needed to have *1) sales skills, 2) product knowledge and 3) a good image.*

"Hmm", I thought, "wonder if there are other examples out there of things that work in threes?" So, some 40 years later, I have researched and discovered that many, many things work in threes. What this message was telling me is that to achieve success or balance in any significant area of my life, the three things that area consisted of had to be present continuously. That's when I had my epiphany. This discovery was telling me the secret to how life <u>really</u> works.

Tryune is a play on the word "triune" as an invitation to "try" this concept. Furthermore, we do not say that life <u>only</u> works in threes. Life also works in ones, twos, fours and so on. What has been observed though is that the many things significant to life, just so happen to come and work in threes. That's what is being shared in this book.

Now, you are about to see 40+ years of research and proof that life works in threes. I did not make up any of these topics. I invite you to research them on the internet to validate what is written here. There are some interesting facts that most of us have never realized...until now.

How Life Works in Threes (around 200 examples)

<u>**LIFE**</u>

Humans consist of *body, mind and soul.*

A human's basic needs are *health, income and provisions.*

A human's basic wants are *comfort, gain and approval.*

Our minds are made up of the *conscious, the subconscious and the unconscious.*

Philosophy explains *the id, the ego and superego.*

Atoms consist of *protons, neutrons and electrons.*

Motion is explained by *three basic laws.*

Science falls under three main branches: *natural, social and formal sciences*

Time is *past, present and future…*at the same time.

Electricity consists of *ohms, amperes and voltage.*

Music's basic elements are *duration, pitch and timbre.*

Democracy is a government *of the people, by the people and for the people.*

U.S. branches of government are *the judicial, the executive and the legislative.*

Armed Forces protect us on *land, air and sea.*

Environmentally, we are asked *to reduce, recycle and re-use.*

The news program gives us *the news, sports and conditions.*

Our days consist of *morning, afternoon and evening.*

Three months in each season of the year

Our main meals are known as *breakfast, lunch and dinner.*

A balanced diet consists of *good proteins, carbohydrates and fats.*

Traditional Family consists of *father, mother, and child(ren)*

<u>SCIENCES</u>

Three major branches of natural science – *(physical, earth/ space and life sciences)*

Three major branches of modern physics - *(classical, relativistic, quantum)*

Three major branches of biology *(botany, zoology, microbiology)*

Three spatial dimensions: *height* (up/down), *width* (left/ right) and *depth* (forwards/backwards)

Three-gauge bosons (photon, gluon, W&Z bosons)

Three types of elementary particles *(leptons, quarks, gauge bosons)*

Three quarks in every proton *(two "up" and one "down")*

Three primary colors of light *(red, green, blue)*

Three color tone properties *(hue, value, chroma)*

Three laws of motion *(Newton's laws)*

Three laws of planetary motion *(Kepler's laws)*

Three layers of the Sun's interior *(core, radiative zone, convective zone)*

Three layers of the Sun's atmosphere *(photosphere, chromosphere, corona)*

Three types of meteorites *(iron, stony iron, stony)*

Three types of galaxy shapes *(elliptical, spiral, irregular)*

Three substances of the universe *(normal matter, 'dark matter', 'dark energy')*

Three phases of the moon *(new moon, first quarter, full moon)*

Three planetary regions *(temperate, sub-tropical, tropical)*

Three layers of the Earth *(crust, mantle, core)*

Three components of an ecosystem *(producers, consumers, decomposers)*

Three types of rocks *(igneous, sedimentary, metamorphic)*

Three types of fossil fuels *(coal, crude oil, natural gas)*

Three hydrological processes *(evaporation, condensation, precipitation)*

Three basic types of (meteorological) precipitation *(liquid, freezing, frozen)*

Three types of substances *(mono-constituent, multi-constituent, UVCB)*

Three phases of (normal) matter (*solid, liquid, gas*)

Three types of covalent chemical bonds (*single, double and triple bonds*)

Three isotopes of hydrogen (*protium, deuterium, tritium*)

Three atoms in each molecule of water (*two hydrogen atoms and an oxygen atom*)

Three endings to salts (*-ide, -ite, -ate*)

Three requirements for fire (*fuel, oxygen, heat*)

Three nucleotide bases in a genetic codon

Three domains of life (*archaea, bacteria and eukaryotes*)

Three major groups of flowering plants (*monocots, eudicots, magnolids*)

Three major functions that are basic to plant growth and development: (*photosynthesis* [making sugars], *respiration* [metabolizing those sugars], and *transpiration* [water vapor loss]

Three things that the chlorophyll in plants needs for photosynthesis to take place: (*sunlight, carbon dioxide and water*)

Transpiration serves three roles: (*cooling the plant, moving minerals* and *sugars through the plant,* and *maintaining the turgidity pressure* [stiffness] *of the plant's cells*)

Three parts of an insect's body (*head, thorax, abdomen*)

BIOLOGY

Three types of cones in the retina, relating to the three primary colors

Three semi-circular canals in the ear *(lateral, anterior, posterior)*

Three sections in the ear *(outer, middle, inner)*

Three ossicles in the middle ear *(malleus, incus, stapes)*

Three segments to each limb *(proximal, mid, distal)*

Three bones in each arm *(humerus, radius, ulna)*

Three joints in the arm *(shoulder, elbow, wrist)*

Three joints in the leg *(hip, knee, ankle)*

Three joints in the elbow *(humeroulnar, humeroradial, proximal radioulnar)*

Three functional compartments in the knee joint *(the femoropatellar, medial femorotibial* and *lateral femorotibial articulations)*

Three types of fibrous joints *(sutures, gomphoses, syndesmoses)*

Three types of bone in each hand *(carpals, metacarpals, phalanges)*

Three types of bone in each foot *(tarsals, metatarsals, phalanges)*

Three bones (phalanges) in each finger and in each toe (*proximal, intermediate, distal*)

Three layers of skin (*dermis, epidermis, hypodermis*)

Three components of a cell (*cell membrane, nucleus, cytoplasm*)

Three types of blood vessels (*arteries, veins, capillaries*)

Three types of blood cells [*red* (erythrocytes), *white* (leukocytes), *platelets* (thrombocytes)]

Three processes of the intestinal tract (*ingestion, digestion, excretion*)

Three germ layers (*Endoderm, Mesoderm, Ectoderm*)

Three parts of a human tooth (*crown, neck, root*)

Three organs of otolaryngology (*ear, nose, throat*)

Three major body systems (*digestive, circulatory, respiratory*)

Three parts to a neuron: (*soma* [*cell body*], *axon, dendrites*)

Three main parts of the brain (*forebrain, midbrain, hindbrain*)

Three parts of the forebrain (*cerebrum, thalamus, hypothalamus*)

Three parts of the midbrain (*colliculi, tegmentum, cerebral peduncles*)

Three parts of the hindbrain (*cerebellum, pons, medulla*)

Three membranes enclosing the brain (*dura mater, arachnoid, pia mater*)

The brain operates on three levels: *consciously* (for cognitive thought and declarative memory); *subconsciously* (for pre-planned actions and procedural memory); and *unconsciously* (for breathing, heart beating, etc.)

Our conscious mind is fed from three sources: *our senses* (which can be fooled); *our memory* (which is flawed); and *our imagination* (which is inventive)

Three aspects of the human mind (*memory, intellect, will*)

Three parts of the human personality (*id, ego, superego*)

The sum of human capacity consists of three abilities (*thought, word and deed*)

Three times of man (*birth, life, death*)

Three periods of the Gait Cycle (*initial double limb support, single limb support, and terminal double limb support*)

<u>MUSIC</u>

Three types of musical notes (*sharps, flats, naturals*)

Three aspects of a song (*lyrics, melody, rhythm*)

Three types of musical chords (*root, third, fifth*)

<u>MATHEMATICS</u>

Three types of a real number (*positive, negative, zero*)

Three parts to any arithmetic operation: for addition: *augend, addend and sum* - for subtraction: *minuend, subtrahend and difference* - for multiplication: *multiplicand, multiplier and product* - for division: *dividend, divisor and quotient*

Three laws of arithmetic operations (*commutative, associative, distributive*)

Three types of equivalence relation (*reflexivity, symmetry, transitivity*)

Three types of symmetry operations (*translation, rotation, reflection*)

Three geometries (*Euclidean, spherical, hyperbolic*)

The number 3 is the basis of an entire branch of mathematics, called trigonometry (from the Greek *trigonon* "triangle" + *metron* "measure")

Three trigonometric functions (*sine, cosine, tangent*)

Three types of average (*mean, mode, median*)

<u>GRAMMAR</u>

Three logical operators (*AND, OR and NOT*)

Three laws of logic (*identity, noncontradiction, excluded middle*)

Three parts of a logical syllogism (*major premise, minor premise, conclusion*)

Three grammatical parts to a sentence (*subject, verb, complement*)

Three persons in grammar [*1st person* (I/we), *2nd* (you or your), *3rd* (he/she/it/they)]

Three genders in grammar [*masculine* (he/him), *feminine* (she/her), *neuter* (it)]

Three forms of comparison in grammar [*positive, comparative* (more, -er), *superlative* (most, -est)]

Three cases in (English) grammar [*subjective/nominative* (he), *objective/accusative* (him) and *possessive/genitive* (his)]

Three parts of a narrative (*beginning, middle, end*)

Components of an essay (*introduction, body, conclusion*)

Elements of a rhetorical appeal (*ethos, pathos, logos*)

Aspects of a story (*plot, characters, setting*)

<u>RELIGION</u>

The Creator – *omniscient, omnipotent, omnipresent*

Christian God – *Father, Son, Holy Spirit*

Jesus – *The Way, The Truth, The Life*

Ancient Near East- *Qudshu, Astarte, Anat*

Classical Antiquity – Many dieties came in threes

Hinduism – Para Brahman is *Brahma, Visnu, Shiva*

Ancient Celtic Cultures – *many example of triad dieties*

Buddhism – *The three jewels*

Taoism – *The three pure ones*

Islam – *Fear, Hope and Love*

Baha'i - *Intention, Power and Action*

Confucianism – *Benevolence, Wisdom and Courage*

OTHER TRIUNE EXAMPLES

3 Coins in a Fountain

3 Days of the Condor

3 Miles in a League

3 Goals in a Hat Trick

3 Piece Suit

3 Feet in a Yard

3 Books in Lord of the Rings

3 Ring Circus

3 Ships of Christopher Columbus

3 Sheets to the Wind

3 Books in a Trilogy

3 Wheels on a Tricycle

3 Wise Men

3-Legged Race

3 Ring Circus

3-Wheeler

3 Cornered Hat

3 Dimensional

3 Musketeers

3 R's (reading, 'riting, 'rithmatic)

3 Sides of a triangle

3 Races in the Triple Crown (horse racing)

3 Angles in a Triangle

3 Trimesters in a Pregnancy

3 Flavors in Neapolitan Ice Cream

3 Stars in Orion's belt

3 Barleycorns in an Inch

3 Hands on a Clock (with the Seconds Hand)

3 Colors in a Flag

3 Minute Egg

3 Great Pyramids at Giza

3 Holes in a Bowling Ball

3 Colors in a Set of Traffic Lights

3 Minutes in a Boxing Round

3 Teaspoons in a Tablespoon

3 Legs on a Stool

3 Monastic Vows (Obience, Stability, Conversatio Morum)

3 Body Types: Endomorph, Mesomorph, Ectomorph

3 Ring Notebooks

3 Germ layers: Endoderm, Mesoderm, Ectoderm

3 Species of Homo: Homo habilis, Homo erectus, Homo sapiens

3 Basic parts of a camera: Lens, Shutter, Sensor

3 Stages of a Project lifecycle: initiation, planning, execution

The Truth, The Whole Truth and Nothing but the Truth

Life, Liberty and the Pursuit of Happiness

Hear no Evil, See no Evil, Speak no Evil

National motto of France/Haiti: Liberty, Equality, Fraternity

Paper, Rock, Scissors

Ready, Aim, Fire

On Your mark, Get Set, Go

Olympic medals of gold, silver, bronze

Types of joints (ball & socket, hinge, pivot)

Stages of a rocket launch (launch, orbit, re-entry)

Parts of a joke (setup, delivery, punchline)

Primary components of a transistor (emitter, base, collector)

Primary components of an airplane (fuselage, wings, empennage)

Basic components of a computer: CPU, memory, storage

Three phases in the development of technology (*eotechnic* [*mechanical*], *paleotechnic* [*steam-powered*] and *neotechnic* [*electric-powered*]

Communication systems require three components (*transmitter, channel, receiver*)

The list goes on. See if you can find more examples as they are everywhere in our universe! Now that you know that life works in threes (with proof!), we can begin to apply this concept to whatever topics we want.

So, to overcome struggles with addiction, we need to apply the three areas that addiction recovery consists of – ACKNOWLEDGE/ACCEPT, SEEK HELP and RECOVERY PLAN. Let's get started!

ACKNOWLEDGE
/ACCEPT
ADDICTION
SEEK
HELP
RECOVERY
PLAN

ADDICTION

Overcoming addiction is a complex process, but here are three significant steps that can help guide you through:

1. **Acknowledgment and Acceptance**: Recognize and accept that you have an addiction. This is often the hardest step but is crucial. It involves being honest with yourself about the impact of the addiction on your life and acknowledging that you need help to make a change.
2. **Seek Professional Help and Build a Support Network**: Reach out to healthcare professionals, such as therapists or addiction specialists, who can provide guidance and treatment options. Additionally, surrounding yourself with a supportive network of friends, family, or support groups can offer encouragement and accountability.
3. **Develop and Implement a Plan for Recovery**: Work with professionals to create a structured plan tailored to your needs. This might include therapy, medication, lifestyle changes, and coping strategies. Consistency and commitment to this plan are key to long-term recovery.

Each of these steps involves commitment and effort, and the journey may vary for each individual.

Addiction can manifest in various forms, affecting both substances and behaviors. Here's a list of different types of addictions:

<u>Substance Addictions:</u>

1. **Alcohol Addiction (Alcoholism)**: Compulsive consumption of alcoholic beverages despite negative consequences.
2. **Drug Addiction**: This includes dependence on:
3. **Opioids** (e.g., heroin, prescription painkillers)

4. **Stimulants** (e.g., cocaine, methamphetamine)
5. **Depressants** (e.g., benzodiazepines, barbiturates)
6. **Hallucinogens** (e.g., LSD, psilocybin mushrooms)
7. **Cannabis** (e.g., marijuana)

Behavioral Addictions:

1. **Gambling Addiction**: Compulsive gambling that disrupts personal and professional life.
2. **Internet Addiction**: Excessive use of the internet that interferes with daily functioning, including social media, gaming, and online activities.
3. **Shopping Addiction (Compulsive Buying Disorder)**: An overwhelming urge to shop and spend, often leading to financial and emotional problems.
4. **Sex Addiction**: Compulsive engagement in sexual activities despite negative consequences.
5. **Food Addiction**: Compulsive overeating or unhealthy eating patterns that impact physical and mental health.
6. **Work Addiction (Workaholism)**: Excessive focus on work at the expense of personal life and well-being.
7. **Exercise Addiction**: Obsessive engagement in physical exercise, often to the detriment of health and social life.
8. **Self-Harm Addiction**: Compulsive engagement in self-injurious behaviors, such as cutting.

Each type of addiction has its own set of challenges and requires a tailored approach to treatment and recovery.

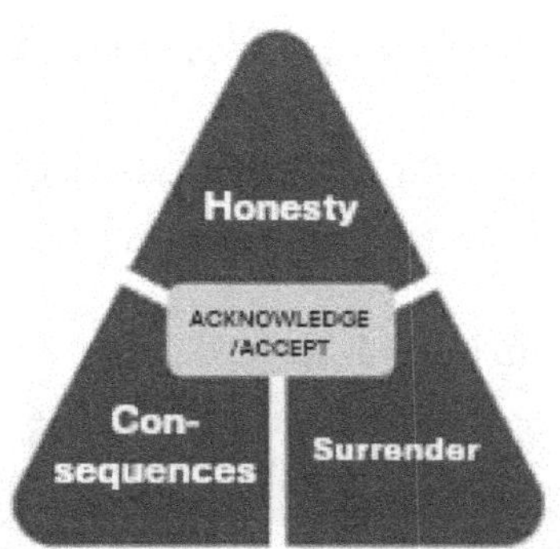

Honesty
ACKNOWLEDGE /ACCEPT
Con-sequences
Surrender

ACKNOWLEDGE/ACCEPT

Acknowledging and accepting an addiction is a crucial first step towards recovery. Here are three key elements to this process:

1. **Self-Reflection and Honest Assessment**: Engage in deep self-reflection to recognize the impact of the addiction on your life. This involves assessing how the substance or behavior affects your health, relationships, and daily functioning. It's important to be honest with yourself about the extent of the problem and to acknowledge any denial or minimization of the issue. This self-awareness is critical for understanding the need for change and seeking help.

2. **Recognize the Consequences**: Identify and accept the negative consequences that the addiction has brought into your life. This includes physical health issues, emotional distress, financial problems, legal troubles, and strained relationships. Acknowledging these impacts can help you grasp the seriousness of the addiction and the urgency of seeking professional treatment.

3. **Acceptance of Vulnerability and Need for Help**: Understand that needing help is not a sign of weakness but a necessary step toward recovery. Acceptance involves recognizing that overcoming addiction often requires support from professionals, such as therapists or addiction specialists, and from a supportive network of friends and family. Embracing this vulnerability can help you overcome any stigma or pride that might be preventing you from seeking the necessary treatment and support. *Basically, it's surrendering to addiction*.

These steps can help build a solid foundation for starting the recovery journey and making meaningful progress toward a healthier, addiction-free life.

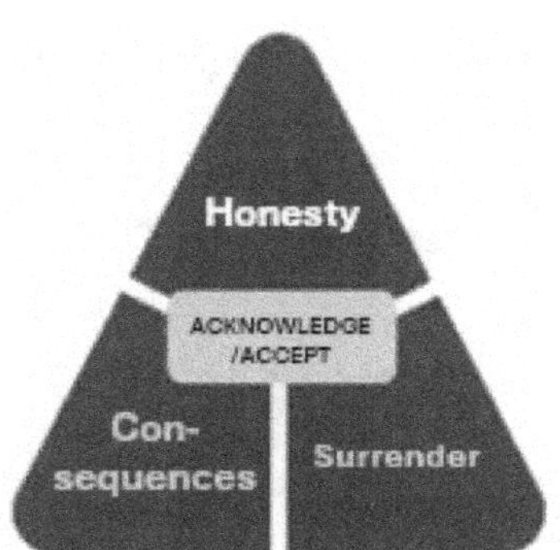

Honesty
ACKNOWLEDGE
/ACCEPT
Con-
sequences
Surrender

Honesty

Being honest with oneself about addiction is a pivotal element in the journey to recovery. This self-honesty requires a clear-eyed evaluation of how the addiction has permeated various aspects of life. It involves confronting uncomfortable truths about the extent of the addiction, including its impacts on health, relationships, and daily responsibilities. This level of honesty means acknowledging that the problem is more than just a minor inconvenience; it's a significant issue that needs addressing. Without this crucial step, denial can cloud judgment and hinder the effectiveness of any recovery efforts.

Furthermore, self-honesty allows individuals to recognize and confront their own patterns of behavior and thinking that contribute to the addiction. This might include identifying triggers that lead to substance use or compulsive behavior, as well as understanding the emotional or psychological needs that the addiction is masking. By facing these underlying factors, individuals can begin to address the root causes of their addiction, rather than just managing symptoms. This deeper insight is essential for developing a comprehensive and effective treatment plan.

Embracing self-honesty also involves accepting that seeking help is a strength, not a weakness. It means acknowledging that overcoming addiction often requires professional intervention, support from loved ones, and a willingness to make significant lifestyle changes. This acceptance helps to dismantle any pride or stigma associated with addiction and opens the door to receiving the necessary support and resources for recovery. Ultimately, being honest with oneself about addiction lays the groundwork for meaningful progress and lasting change.

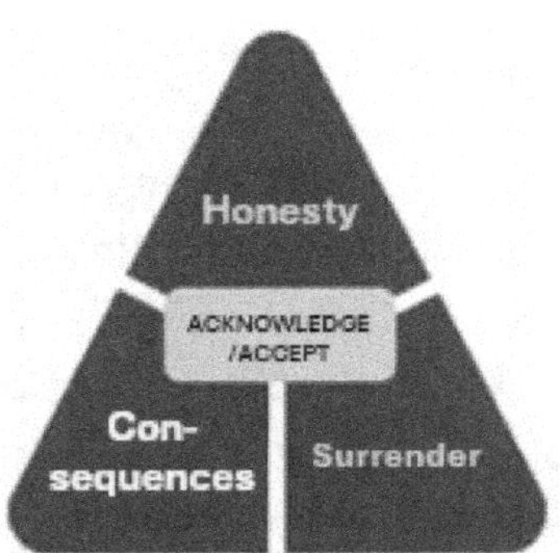
Honesty
ACKNOWLEDGE
/ACCEPT
Con-
sequences
Surrender

Consequences

Failing to seek help for an addiction can have severe and wide-ranging consequences that affect almost every aspect of an individual's life. Physically, the continued use of addictive substances or engagement in compulsive behaviors can lead to deteriorating health. This includes chronic diseases, such as liver damage from alcohol abuse, heart problems from stimulant use, or severe nutritional deficiencies from disordered eating. These health issues not only shorten life expectancy but also diminish quality of life, leading to frequent medical complications and a decline in overall well-being.

Emotionally and psychologically, not addressing an addiction often exacerbates feelings of guilt, shame, and hopelessness. The cycle of addiction can lead to worsening mental health issues, such as anxiety, depression, or even suicidal thoughts. The temporary relief or pleasure gained from the addiction is overshadowed by an increasing sense of emotional despair. This emotional strain can create a vicious cycle where the individual uses the substance or behavior more intensely to escape their feelings, which in turn worsens their emotional state.

Socially and relationally, addiction can erode trust and strain relationships with family, friends, and colleagues. The behaviors associated with addiction often lead to dishonesty, broken promises, and conflicts that drive wedges between individuals and their loved ones. This social isolation can further exacerbate addiction, as the lack of supportive relationships leaves individuals without crucial sources of encouragement and accountability. Over time, the combination of health decline, emotional distress, and damaged relationships can severely limit one's personal and professional opportunities, making recovery increasingly difficult.

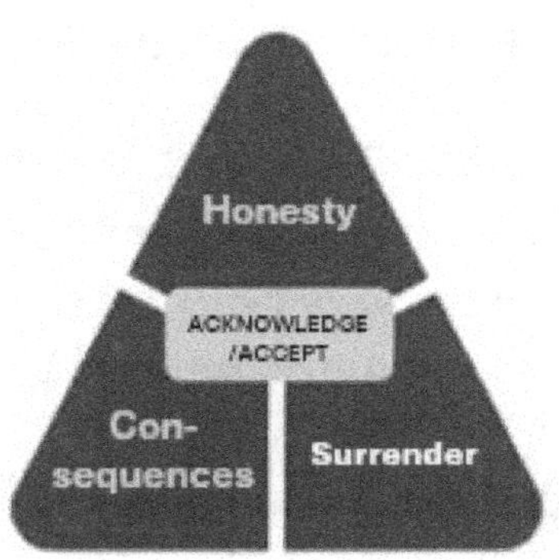
Honesty
ACKNOWLEDGE
/ACCEPT
Con-
sequences
Surrender

Surrender

Surrendering to an addiction is a vital step on the road to recovery, as it marks the moment when an individual fully acknowledges their inability to control the addiction on their own. This surrender involves letting go of the illusion of self-control and admitting that professional help and support are essential. By accepting that addiction has taken over their life and recognizing their powerlessness over it, individuals can shift from a mindset of denial to one of acceptance. This admission is not a sign of weakness but rather a courageous and necessary step toward seeking and receiving the help required for recovery.

The act of surrendering also opens the door to new strategies and support systems that can facilitate healing. When individuals admit they cannot overcome their addiction alone, they become more receptive to various forms of assistance, including therapy, counseling, support groups, and medical treatment. This openness allows them to learn and implement new coping strategies, gain insights into their behavior, and benefit from the experiences of others who have faced similar struggles. Surrendering creates a willingness to engage in a structured recovery process, which can significantly enhance the chances of long-term success.

Moreover, surrendering to an addiction fosters a sense of humility and self-compassion. It helps individuals move beyond self-blame and frustration, allowing them to approach their recovery journey with a more constructive and hopeful mindset. This shift in perspective can lead to greater emotional resilience and a more balanced view of oneself. Embracing this humility can also improve interpersonal relationships, as individuals become more open to honest communication and rebuilding trust with loved ones. In essence, surrendering to an addiction is a profound and transformative step that paves the way for meaningful change and a more hopeful path toward recovery.

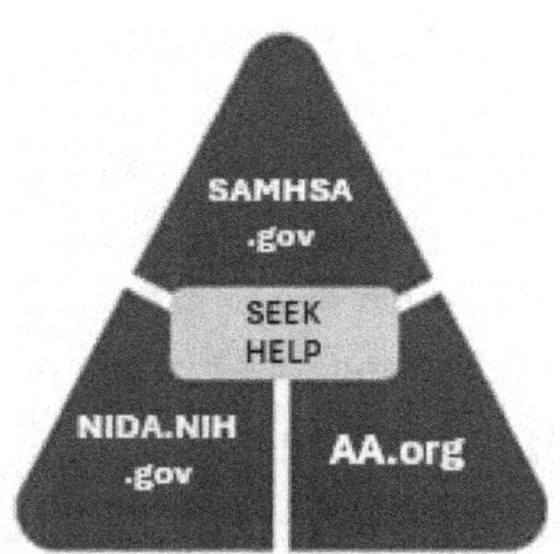
SAMHSA
.gov
SEEK
HELP
NIDA.NIH
.gov
AA.org

SEEK HELP

Seeking outside help with addiction is essential because addiction often involves complex physiological and psychological components that are challenging to address alone. Professional treatment provides access to medical and therapeutic expertise that can address the underlying causes of addiction, such as imbalances in brain chemistry, co-occurring mental health disorders, or trauma. Specialized treatment programs offer evidence-based interventions, including medication-assisted treatment, cognitive-behavioral therapy, and motivational interviewing, which are designed to target the specific needs of individuals struggling with addiction. These resources help manage withdrawal symptoms, reduce cravings, and provide strategies for long-term recovery.

In addition to medical and psychological support, outside help brings the benefit of structured guidance and accountability. Addiction recovery often requires significant lifestyle changes and the development of new coping strategies. Professionals, such as therapists and addiction counselors, can offer structured programs and frameworks that guide individuals through these changes systematically. Support groups and recovery communities also play a critical role by providing a network of peers who understand the challenges of addiction. This social support offers encouragement, accountability, and shared experiences that can significantly enhance the recovery process.

Moreover, seeking external help helps to counteract the isolation that often accompanies addiction. Individuals struggling with addiction may feel alone and disconnected from their support networks due to the nature of their behavior or the stigma associated with addiction. Reaching out for help connects individuals to a broader support system that includes family, friends, and other recovering individuals. This sense of community and connection can foster a more positive and hopeful outlook, which is crucial for sustaining motivation and commitment to the recovery journey. By seeking outside help, individuals gain access to a comprehensive support system that enhances their chances of achieving and maintaining long-term sobriety.

When seeking support for addiction, accessing reliable resources can be crucial for effective treatment and recovery. Here are three valuable sources:

1. **Substance Abuse and Mental Health Services Administration (SAMHSA)**

Website: SAMHSA.gov

Description: SAMHSA is a U.S. government agency that provides comprehensive information on substance abuse and mental health. Their website offers resources for finding treatment services, understanding various types of addiction, and accessing support groups. They also provide a national helpline that can connect individuals to local treatment resources.

1. **National Institute on Drug Abuse (NIDA)**

Website: NIDA.NIH.gov

Description: NIDA is a leading research organization focused on drug abuse and addiction. Their website provides evidence-based information about the science of addiction, treatment options, and prevention strategies. It also features educational materials for individuals and families seeking to understand and address addiction.

1. **Alcoholics Anonymous (AA)**

Website: AA.org

Description: AA is a well-known support group for individuals struggling with alcohol addiction. The organization offers a 12-step program and provides resources for finding local meetings and support groups. AA's approach focuses on peer support and shared experiences, which can be invaluable in the recovery process.

These sources offer a mix of professional, scientific, and peer-based support that can be instrumental in the journey to recovery.

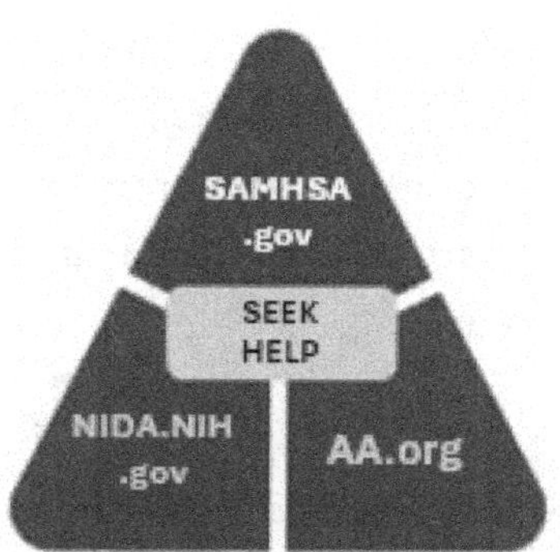

SAMHSA
.gov
SEEK
HELP
NIDA.NIH
.gov
AA.org

SAMHSA.gov

SAMHSA.gov, the website of the Substance Abuse and Mental Health Services Administration, offers a wide range of services designed to support individuals struggling with substance abuse and mental health issues. One of the key services provided is the **National Helpline**, also known as the **Treatment Referral Routing Service**. This confidential, 24/7 helpline connects individuals to local treatment facilities, support groups, and community resources. The helpline can provide immediate assistance and guidance, helping individuals navigate the often-overwhelming process of finding appropriate care and support.

In addition to direct support through the helpline, SAMHSA.gov provides **extensive educational resources** and **publications** on a variety of topics related to substance abuse and mental health. Their website features comprehensive information on different types of addictions, treatment approaches, prevention strategies, and the science behind mental health and substance use disorders. These resources are valuable for both individuals seeking help and professionals looking for up-to-date information and best practices in the field of addiction treatment.

SAMHSA.gov also offers a range of **grant programs** and **funding opportunities** aimed at supporting community-based initiatives and organizations dedicated to addressing substance abuse and mental health issues. These grants help fund programs that provide prevention, treatment, and recovery services across various communities. By supporting these initiatives, SAMHSA contributes to the development and sustainability of effective programs that improve access to care and support for individuals facing addiction and mental health challenges.

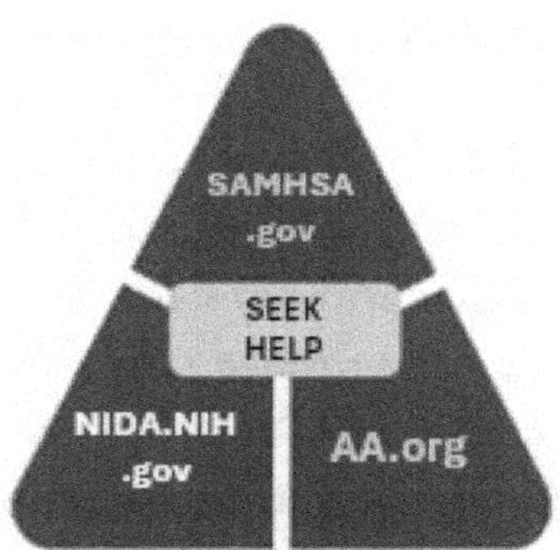

SAMHSA
.gov
SEEK
HELP
NIDA.NIH
.gov
AA.org

NIDA.NIH.gov

The National Institute on Drug Abuse (NIDA) website offers a wealth of **educational resources** focused on the science of drug abuse and addiction. NIDA provides in-depth information on various substances, including their effects on the brain and body, the risk factors for addiction, and the latest research findings. These resources are designed to enhance public understanding and awareness of addiction, offering valuable insights for individuals, families, and educators. By disseminating current scientific knowledge, NIDA helps to educate the public about the complexities of addiction and the importance of evidence-based approaches to treatment and prevention.

NIDA also offers detailed **information on treatment options** and **recovery strategies**. Their website provides guidance on the various methods available for treating drug addiction, including medication-assisted treatment, behavioral therapies, and support systems. This includes practical advice on how to seek treatment, what to expect during the recovery process, and how to access resources for ongoing support. By outlining these treatment modalities and their efficacy, NIDA helps individuals and healthcare providers make informed decisions about the best approaches to managing and overcoming addiction.

Furthermore, NIDA supports **research and funding opportunities** through its website, which are crucial for advancing the understanding and treatment of addiction. The institute funds research projects and initiatives aimed at discovering new treatments, improving existing therapies, and exploring innovative prevention strategies. This commitment to research ensures that the field of addiction treatment continues to evolve based on the latest scientific evidence. NIDA's emphasis on research not only advances the knowledge base but also contributes to the development of effective, evidence-based practices that benefit those struggling with addiction and mental health issues.

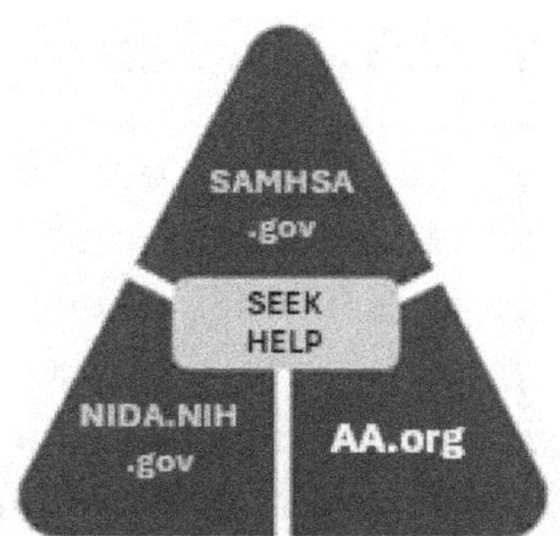

SAMHSA
.gov
SEEK
HELP
NIDA.NIH
.gov
AA.org

AA.org

The Alcoholics Anonymous (AA) website offers a range of **support and recovery resources** designed to assist individuals struggling with alcohol addiction. One of the primary services provided is access to **local AA meetings**. The website features a searchable database that helps users find meetings in their area, whether they are looking for in-person, virtual, or phone meetings. This accessibility ensures that individuals seeking support can find a meeting that fits their schedule and needs, fostering a sense of community and connection that is essential for recovery.

AA.org also provides extensive **educational materials** about the 12-step program and the principles of Alcoholics Anonymous. These resources include literature such as "The Big Book," which outlines the foundational principles of the AA program and shares personal stories of recovery. The website offers information on how the 12-step approach works, the philosophy behind it, and its effectiveness in supporting long-term sobriety. This educational content helps individuals understand the AA approach and prepare for their recovery journey.

In addition to meeting information and educational materials, AA.org offers **resources for getting involved** and supporting the fellowship. This includes opportunities for individuals to participate in service roles, contribute to the organization, and engage in various AA-related activities. The site also provides guidance on starting new AA groups and maintaining existing ones, ensuring that the AA network continues to grow and support more individuals in their recovery. By offering these services, AA.org helps individuals not only find support but also become active participants in the recovery community, reinforcing their commitment to sobriety and helping others along the way.

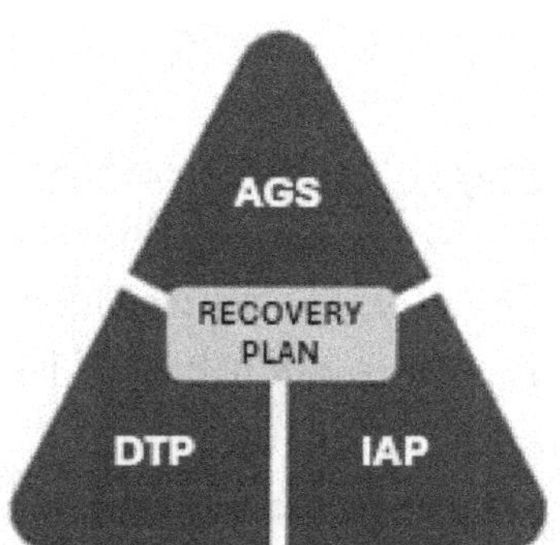
AGS
RECOVERY
PLAN
DTP
IAP

RECOVERY PLAN

Creating a recovery plan for addiction involves several key steps to ensure a structured and effective approach. Here are three crucial steps for developing a comprehensive recovery plan:

1. **Assessment and Goal Setting:**

Assessment: Begin by conducting a thorough self-assessment or seek a professional evaluation to understand the extent of the addiction and identify any co-occurring mental health issues. This step helps in understanding the specific needs and challenges related to your addiction.

Goal Setting: Establish clear, realistic, and measurable goals for your recovery. These goals should include short-term objectives, such as reducing substance use or attending support meetings regularly, and long-term goals, like achieving sustained sobriety and rebuilding personal relationships. Setting goals provides direction and motivation throughout the recovery journey.

1. **Developing a Treatment Plan:**

Professional Treatment: Engage with healthcare professionals to create a tailored treatment plan. This may involve a combination of medication-assisted treatment, therapy (e.g., cognitive-behavioral therapy), and counseling. The plan should address both the physical and psychological aspects of addiction and provide strategies for managing cravings and avoiding relapse.

Support Network: Incorporate support from family, friends, and support groups, such as Alcoholics Anonymous (AA) or Narcotics Anonymous (NA). Building a strong support network offers encouragement, accountability, and shared experiences that are vital for recovery.

1. **Implementing and Adjusting the Plan**:
    ◦ **Action and Routine**: Implement the treatment plan and establish a daily routine that supports recovery. This includes attending therapy sessions, participating in support groups, and engaging in healthy activities that promote well-being. Consistency and commitment to these activities are key to making progress.
    ◦ **Monitoring and Adjustment**: Regularly review and adjust the recovery plan as needed. Monitor progress toward goals and be open to making changes based on what is or isn't working. This might involve modifying treatment approaches, seeking additional support, or addressing new challenges that arise. Flexibility and ongoing evaluation help ensure that the recovery plan remains effective and responsive to evolving needs.

These steps provide a structured approach to managing addiction, focusing on assessment, treatment, and continuous improvement to support long-term recovery.

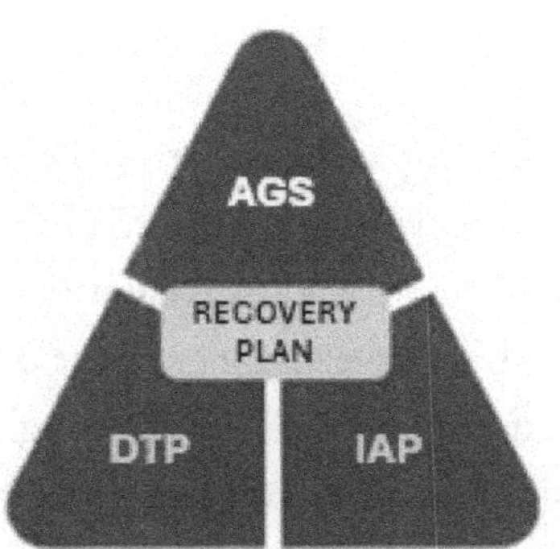
AGS
RECOVERY
PLAN
DTP
IAP

AGS

Assessment and goal setting are foundational elements in the recovery process from addiction, providing a clear roadmap for overcoming the challenges of addiction. The initial assessment involves a comprehensive evaluation of the addiction's severity, its impact on physical and mental health, and any co-occurring issues. This thorough understanding helps identify the specific needs and triggers associated with addiction, allowing for the development of a personalized and effective treatment plan. By recognizing the full scope of the problem, individuals and professionals can address both the addiction itself and any underlying factors that contribute to it.

Goal setting is equally critical, as it provides direction and motivation throughout the recovery journey. Setting clear, realistic, and measurable goals helps individuals focus on specific aspects of their recovery, such as reducing substance use, improving mental health, or repairing relationships. Short-term goals offer immediate targets to strive for, while long-term goals provide a vision for sustained recovery and personal growth. This structured approach not only helps maintain motivation but also allows individuals to track their progress and celebrate milestones, reinforcing positive behavior and enhancing the likelihood of long-term success.

Moreover, assessment and goal setting facilitate the creation of a structured and actionable recovery plan. By evaluating progress and adjusting goals as needed, individuals can address challenges and adapt to changes in their recovery journey. This flexibility is essential for overcoming obstacles and maintaining momentum. Regular reviews of both the assessment and goals ensure that the recovery plan remains relevant and effective, providing ongoing support and guidance as individuals work towards a healthier, addiction-free life.

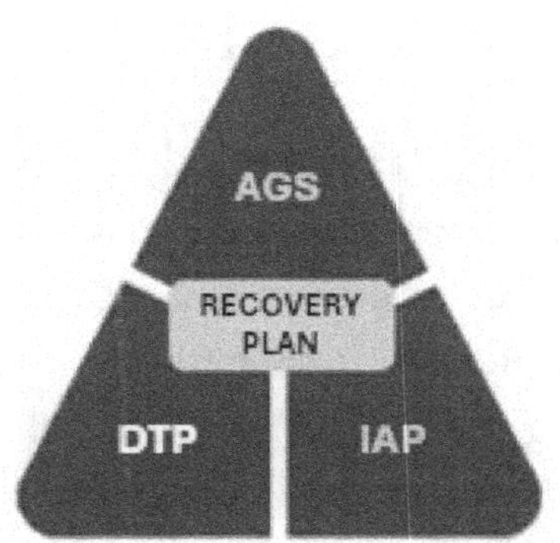
AGS
RECOVERY
PLAN
DTP
IAP

DTP

Developing a treatment plan is crucial for addiction recovery as it provides a structured approach to addressing both the physical and psychological aspects of addiction. A well-crafted treatment plan outlines specific strategies and interventions tailored to an individual's unique needs, ensuring a comprehensive approach to recovery. This plan typically includes a combination of medical treatment, such as medication-assisted therapy, and psychological support, such as counseling and cognitive-behavioral therapy. By addressing the root causes of addiction and implementing evidence-based strategies, the treatment plan helps individuals manage withdrawal symptoms, reduce cravings, and develop healthier coping mechanisms.

In addition, a treatment plan establishes clear goals and benchmarks for progress, which are essential for maintaining motivation and accountability. By setting specific, measurable objectives, individuals can track their progress and recognize their achievements, no matter how small. This structured approach helps to reinforce commitment to recovery and provides a sense of direction and purpose. Regular evaluations of the treatment plan also allow for adjustments based on the individual's progress and evolving needs, ensuring that the approach remains effective and relevant throughout the recovery process.

Moreover, a treatment plan fosters a sense of collaboration between the individual and their healthcare providers. It involves creating a partnership where the individual's preferences, goals, and concerns are taken into account, leading to a more personalized and effective approach to treatment. This collaborative process enhances trust and communication, making it easier for individuals to engage in their recovery journey and adhere to the prescribed treatment. By involving both the individual and their support network in the planning process, a treatment plan ensures a holistic approach that integrates various aspects of care and support, ultimately contributing to a more successful and sustained recovery.

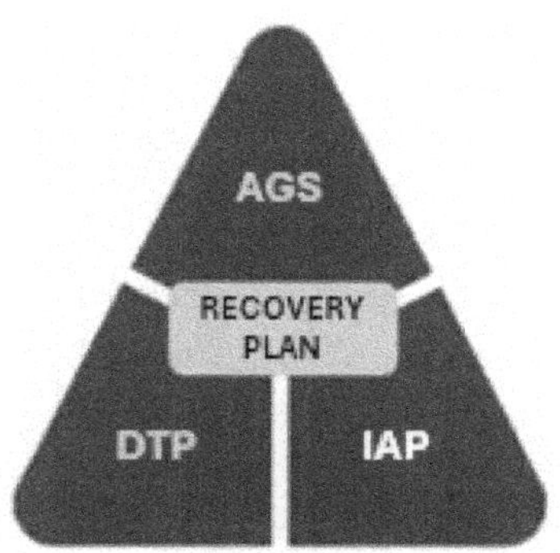
AGS
RECOVERY
PLAN
DTP
IAP

IAP

Implementing and adjusting a plan for addiction recovery is vital because it translates theoretical strategies into actionable steps that guide individuals through their journey towards sobriety. Once a comprehensive treatment plan is developed, it must be put into practice through consistent actions such as attending therapy sessions, participating in support groups, and adhering to prescribed medications. This implementation phase is where the plan becomes a daily routine, helping individuals build new habits, reinforce positive behaviors, and develop coping strategies essential for overcoming addiction. By following the plan, individuals can systematically address the various challenges of recovery, providing structure and discipline in the pursuit of long-term sobriety.

Adjusting the plan as needed is equally crucial for addressing the dynamic nature of addiction recovery. As individuals progress, they may encounter new challenges, experience changes in their circumstances, or discover aspects of their recovery that require modification. Regularly reviewing and adapting the treatment plan ensures that it remains effective and responsive to these evolving needs. This flexibility allows for the incorporation of new strategies, the refinement of existing approaches, and the adjustment of goals based on progress or setbacks. By making necessary adjustments, individuals can stay on track and continue to address issues that arise, enhancing their chances of sustained recovery.

Moreover, the process of adjusting the plan fosters a proactive approach to recovery, encouraging individuals to be actively involved in their own healing process. It empowers them to identify and address potential obstacles before they become significant problems, promoting a sense of ownership and responsibility in their recovery journey. This continuous evaluation and modification also provide opportunities for individuals to learn more about themselves, their triggers, and their coping mechanisms, leading to greater self-awareness and resilience. Overall, implementing and adjusting the recovery plan are essential for maintaining progress, adapting to challenges, and

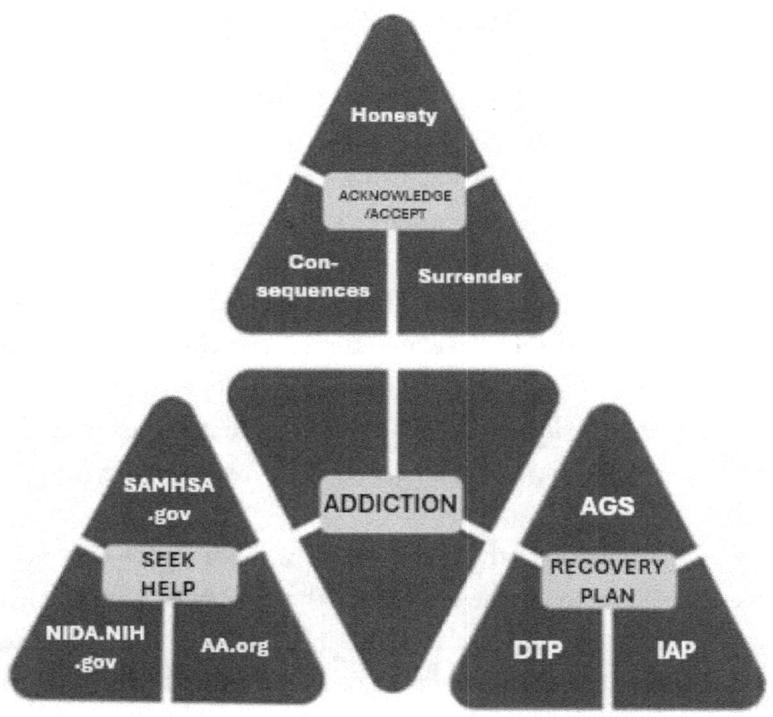
Honesty
ACKNOWLEDGE /ACCEPT
Con-sequences
Surrender
SAMHSA .gov
SEEK HELP
NIDA.NIH .gov
AA.org
ADDICTION
AGS
RECOVERY PLAN
DTP
IAP

SUMMARY

The odds of recovering from addiction vary widely depending on several factors, including the nature of the addiction, the individual's personal circumstances, and the quality of treatment received. Research shows that with appropriate and sustained intervention, a significant proportion of individuals can achieve and maintain long-term sobriety. For example, studies indicate that about one-third of individuals who receive treatment for substance use disorders achieve a substantial reduction in their substance use and improve their overall quality of life. While these statistics suggest a positive outlook, the journey to recovery is highly individualistic and influenced by a range of personal and environmental factors.

Key factors that affect the likelihood of successful recovery include the type and duration of the addiction, the presence of co-occurring mental health conditions, and the individual's support system. Individuals who engage in comprehensive treatment programs that include both medical and psychological support are generally more likely to achieve better outcomes. Additionally, having a strong network of support from family, friends, and peer support groups can significantly enhance the chances of recovery. Addressing co-occurring issues, such as anxiety or depression, through integrated treatment approaches also improves the likelihood of sustained recovery.

However, it is important to recognize that recovery from addiction is often a lifelong process, and relapse can be a part of that journey. The key to improving recovery odds lies in persistence and resilience, as many individuals experience multiple attempts at recovery before achieving long-term success. Effective recovery involves continuous self-care, ongoing support, and adaptive strategies to manage cravings and avoid triggers. While the path to recovery may be challenging, many individuals do succeed and go on to lead fulfilling lives, demonstrating that recovery is possible with the right resources, commitment, and support.

Invitation

If there is one area that I have had a lot of experience with…it would be addiction. Fortunately, I did not have a battle with addiction during my lifetime but those close to me have.

My father and father-in-law battled alcoholism. My father came out of it but unfortunately my father-in-law did not. My best friend from school struggles with drugs and alcohol from his work and is still battling those demons after 40 years. And lastly, my business partner became addicted to opioids that he took for tremendous pain from an accident. Unfortunately, he lost that battle as well.

Needless to say, I had many conversations with all these men that were close to me. What I gleaned from all that experience over 50 years is this:

"You can't reason with a mind that is not reasonable." What that means is that when you're talking with someone who is in the middle of addiction, they are looking at you, but they are not listening to what you are saying, most likely. Their minds are full of chemicals, and they are wondering where they are going to get their next "hit".

The other lesson I learned is that I am not qualified to fix someone. And no matter how much I wanted to help these people, that didn't matter. They must want help and surrender to it. We live in a world of instant gratification, but addiction recovery is a long, hard process for the person with the addiction. Patience is required by all involved.

Quotes about Addiction

- "Addiction is a condition where someone's brain and behavior are hijacked by a substance, leading them to pursue and use it despite its negative impact on their lives."

— Dr. Nora Volkow

- "The greatest glory in living lies not in never falling, but in rising every time we fall."

— Nelson Mandela

- "Recovery is not for people who need it. It's for people who want it."

— Unknown

- "Addiction is not a weakness, it's a sign of something more profound and complex going on inside."

— Dr. Gabor Maté

- "The best way to predict your future is to create it."

— Peter Drucker

- "Recovery is an acceptance that your life is in shambles, and you have to change it."

— Jamie Lee Curtis

- "The first step toward change is awareness. The second step is acceptance."

— Nathaniel Branden

- "You don't have to control your thoughts. You just have to stop letting them control you."

— David Allen

- "It does not matter how slowly you go, as long as you do not stop."

— Confucius

- "When everything seems to be going against you, remember that the airplane takes off against the wind, not with it."

— Henry Ford

Is Addiction a Disease or a Choice?

The debate over whether addiction is a disease, or a choice involves complex considerations, reflecting both the biological and behavioral aspects of addiction. From a medical perspective, addiction is widely recognized as a disease due to its effects on brain function and structure. Neurobiological research has demonstrated that addiction alters the brain's reward system, impairing the ability to make sound decisions and regulate behavior. This understanding aligns with the view of addiction as a chronic, relapsing condition that affects brain chemistry, making it difficult for individuals to control their substance use despite their best intentions. The disease model helps to reduce stigma and emphasizes the need for medical treatment and support for those struggling with addiction.

On the other hand, the perspective that addiction involves elements of personal choice acknowledges the role of individual behavior and decision-making. This view argues that while biological factors contribute to addiction, personal choices and circumstances also play a significant role. Individuals might initially engage in substance use due to various reasons such as peer pressure, stress, or curiosity, and their continued use can be influenced by lifestyle choices, environmental factors, and coping strategies. From this standpoint, recovery involves not only medical and psychological treatment but also personal commitment and active participation in changing one's behavior and lifestyle.

Ultimately, understanding addiction as both a disease and a choice can provide a more comprehensive approach to treatment and recovery. Recognizing addiction as a disease underscores the importance of medical intervention and support, while acknowledging personal choice emphasizes the role of individual agencies in the recovery process. A balanced perspective can foster empathy and support for those affected by addiction, promoting effective treatment strategies that address both the biological and behavioral aspects of the condition. This integrated approach highlights the importance of addressing underlying issues while empowering individuals to make positive changes in their lives.

What is the root cause of addiction?

The root cause of addiction is multifaceted, involving a complex interplay of biological, psychological, and environmental factors. Here's a breakdown of these contributing elements:

1. Biological Factors:

- **Genetics**: Research indicates that genetics can play a significant role in addiction. Individuals with a family history of addiction are at a higher risk due to inherited genetic predispositions that affect the brain's reward system. Certain genes may influence how the brain responds to substances and how susceptible a person is to developing addictive behaviors.
- **Brain Chemistry**: Addiction is associated with changes in brain chemistry and function. Substances and behaviors that are addictive often alter neurotransmitter systems, particularly those involving dopamine and serotonin. These changes can disrupt normal brain function, making it difficult for individuals to control their impulses and behavior.

2. Psychological Factors:

- **Mental Health Conditions**: Co-occurring mental health disorders, such as anxiety, depression, or trauma, can significantly contribute to addiction. Individuals may use substances or engage in addictive behaviors as a means of self-medication to cope with underlying psychological distress or emotional pain.
- **Personality Traits**: Certain personality traits, such as impulsivity, risk-taking behavior, and high levels of stress, can increase the likelihood of developing an addiction. These traits

can influence how individuals respond to stress and seek out substances or behaviors that provide temporary relief or pleasure.

3. Environmental and Social Factors:

- **Family and Peer Influence**: Environmental factors, including family dynamics and peer pressure, can play a crucial role in the development of addiction. Exposure to substance use in the family or social circles, particularly during adolescence, can increase the risk of developing addictive behaviors.
- **Life Circumstances and Stressors**: Stressful life events, such as trauma, abuse, or socioeconomic hardship, can contribute to addiction. Individuals may turn to substances or addictive behaviors as a way to escape or manage these stressors.

Understanding addiction requires acknowledging this intricate web of influences and recognizing that there is no single root cause. Rather, it is the interplay of genetic, psychological, and environmental factors that together contribute to the development and perpetuation of addictive behaviors. Addressing addiction effectively often requires a comprehensive approach that considers all these dimensions and provides tailored interventions to support recovery.

When you're with someone who is sharing their struggles with you...just smile at him/her and give them one of these. He/she will ask "What is that?" Then simply reply "Life Works in Threes."

Other titles coming out:

- Weight Struggles?
- Abundance Struggles?
- Parenting Struggles?
- Life Struggles?
- Purpose Struggles?
- Happiness Struggles?
- Sales Struggles?
- Speaker Struggles?
- Time Struggles?
- Network Struggles?
- Marriage Struggles?
- Divorce Struggles?
- Money Struggles?
- Career Struggles?
- Dating Struggles?
- Caretaker Struggles?
- Forgiveness Struggles?
- Grieving Struggles?
- Success Struggles?
- Golf Struggles?
- Workplace Struggles?
- Stress Struggles?
- Shame/Guilt Struggles?
- Romance Struggles?

Remember,
When you get right down to it,
Life is about making choices.

Every day, all day long, that's what we do.

- *We choose to get out of bed or not.*
- *We choose to clean up or not.*
- *We choose what to eat all day.*
- *We choose to exercise or not.*
- *We choose to go to work or not.*
- *We choose to do a good job or not.*
- *We choose to come home or not.*
- *We choose to watch TV or do something constructive.*
- *We choose to bed at a decent hour or not.*

And the next day...we start all over again.
What is the meaning of this? Get good at choosing.
Before you can get good at choosing though...you need to understand how life works in threes.

When someone is struggling with a particular area or two, chances are they are "out of balance" with how life works. How does life work? Life works in threes.

If you're interested in personal topics like life, health, money or business topics like sales, time management and public speaking...Life Works in Threes! can shed some light on creating success in those areas.

The definition of TRIUNE is a group of three things; united. Being three in one, such as - humans are *mental, physical* and *spiritual beings.* The word TRYUNE is a play of the word TRIUNE, encouraging all to try this concept and help eliminate struggling unnecessarily.

LifeWorksInThrees.com